Cocktails,
Punches & Cups

Hilary Walden

Glühwein

Makes about 6 glasses or mugs
Preparation time: 20 minutes

1 lemon

8 cloves

1 x 75 cl/26.40 fl oz bottle
red wine

100 g/4 oz sugar

2 x 5 cm/2 inch cinnamon sticks

150 ml/¼ pint brandy

1. Spike the lemon with the cloves.
2. Gently heat the wine, sugar, cinnamon sticks and lemon in a saucepan to just below simmering point for 10 minutes.
3. Lower the heat and add the brandy. Warm for 2-3 minutes.
4. Strain and serve immediately in warmed glasses or mugs.

Margarita

Serves 1
Preparation time: 5 minutes

a little lemon juice

finely ground sea salt

1½ measures Tequila

1 measure Triple Sec

1-2 tablespoons lemon or lime
juice

cracked ice

1. Dip the rim of a chilled glass in lemon juice, then in the salt.
2. Place the Tequila, Triple Sec, lemon or lime juice and cracked ice in a cocktail shaker or screw-topped jar. Shake well to mix.
3. Pour into the glass.

Americano

Serves 1
Preparation time: 5 minutes

cracked ice

1 measure Campari

2 measures sweet vermouth

soda water

twist of lemon peel, to decorate

1. Put some cracked ice into a tumbler, pour the Campari and vermouth over. Stir to mix.
2. Top up with soda water to taste. Decorate with the lemon peel.

Black Russian

Serves 1
Preparation time: 5 minutes

cracked ice

2 measures vodka

1 measure Kahlúa coffee liqueur

1. Put some cracked ice in a glass.
2. Pour the vodka and Kahlúa over. Stir to mix.

Bloody Mary

Serves 1
Preparation time: 5 minutes

1 measure vodka

2 measures tomato juice

dash of Worcestershire sauce

squeeze of lemon juice

cracked ice

celery salt, to taste

cayenne pepper, to taste

sprig of mint, to decorate

1. Place the vodka, tomato juice, Worcestershire sauce, lemon juice and cracked ice in a cocktail shaker or screw-topped jar. Shake to mix.
2. Strain into a glass. Add celery salt and cayenne pepper to taste. Decorate with the mint.

Brandy cocktail

Serves 1
Preparation time: 5 minutes

cracked ice

2 measures Cognac or brandy

1 measure Curaçao

To decorate:

twist of lemon peel

1 cocktail cherry

1. Put some cracked ice in a small tumbler or glass.
2. Pour the Cognac and Curaçao over, and stir. Decorate with the lemon peel and cherry.

Bronx

Serves 1
Preparation time: 5 minutes

cracked ice

1 measure gin

1 measure sweet vermouth

1 measure dry vermouth

2 measures fresh orange juice

1. Place some cracked ice, the gin, sweet and dry vermouth and orange juice in a cocktail shaker or screw-topped jar. Shake to mix.
2. Pour into a small glass, straining the drink if preferred.

Daiquiri

Serves 1
Preparation time: 5 minutes

lightly beaten egg white

caster sugar

cracked ice

1 measure lime cordial or juice

3 measures white rum

For a Banana Daiquiri:

cracked ice

1 measure white rum

1 measure dark rum

2 measures orange juice

½ measure banana liqueur

½ small banana

1 measure single cream
   (optional)

To decorate:

2 cocktail cherries

1 slice pineapple

1. Dip the rim of a tumbler in lightly beaten egg white, then in caster sugar.
2. Put some cracked ice into the glass, pour over the lime juice cordial or juice then the rum. Stir lightly. Alternatively, place in a cocktail shaker or screw-topped jar and shake lightly.

1. Put some cracked ice in a glass.
2. Put the other ingredients in a liquidizer until well blended.
3. Pour into the glass and decorate with the cocktail cherries and pineapple, on a cocktail stick.

Edgemoor

Serves 1
Preparation time: 5 minutes

cracked ice

1 measure dark rum

1 measure white rum

1 measure Irish Mist

3 measures fresh pineapple
   juice

1 teaspoon lime cordial

soda water

slices lemon and orange, to
   decorate

1. Place some cracked ice, the rum, Irish Mist, pineapple juice and lime cordial in a cocktail shaker or screw-topped jar. Shake lightly to mix.
2. Strain into a tall glass and top up with soda water to taste. Decorate with lemon and orange slices, twisted together.

Gimlet

Serves 1
Preparation time: 5 minutes

cracked ice

1 measure lime cordial

2 measures gin

soda water (optional)

1 slice cucumber, to decorate

1. Put some cracked ice into a tall glass. Pour the lime cordial over and stir.
2. Add the gin and stir lightly to mix. Top up with soda water to taste, if using.
3. Decorate with the cucumber slice, on a cocktail stick or parasol stick.

Harlequin

Serves 1
Preparation time: 5 minutes

lightly beaten egg white

caster sugar

1 measure Kirsch

1 measure apricot brandy

2 measures fresh orange juice

soda water

To decorate:

1 slice orange

2 cocktail cherries

1. Dip the rim of a tumbler in a lightly beaten egg white, then in caster sugar.
2. Place the Kirsch, apricot brandy and orange juice in a cocktail shaker or screw-topped jar. Shake lightly to mix.
3. Strain into the glass and top up with soda water to taste.
4. Decorate with the orange slice and cherries on a cocktail stick.

Harvey wallbanger

Serves 1
Preparation time: 5 minutes

cracked ice

2 measures fresh orange juice

1 measure vodka

2 teaspoons Galliano

To decorate:

slice of cucumber

twist of orange peel

1 slice pineapple

cocktail cherry

1. Place some cracked ice in a tumbler. Pour on the fresh orange juice and vodka.
2. Pour on the Galliano and stir well. Decorate with the cucumber, orange peel, pineapple and cocktail cherry, on a cocktail stick.

Highball

Serves 1
Preparation time: 5 minutes

cracked ice

1 measure whisky

dry ginger ale

1. Put some cracked ice in a tumbler and pour the whisky over.
2. Top up with the ginger ale to taste.

John Collins

Serves 1
Preparation time: 5 minutes

1 teaspoon caster sugar

1-2 tablespoons lemon juice

cracked ice

1 measure gin

soda water

1 slice lemon

1. Put the sugar into a tumbler, add the lemon juice and stir until the sugar has dissolved.
2. Add some cracked ice and stir well. Add the gin and stir lightly.
3. Add soda water to taste, then decorate the rim of the tumbler with the slice of lemon.

Lion d'or

Serves 1
Preparation time: 5 minutes

cracked ice

2 measures Grand Marnier

1 measure gin

1 measure fresh orange juice

strip of orange peel, to decorate

1. Place some cracked ice, the Grand Marnier, gin and orange juice in a cocktail shaker or screw-topped jar. Shake lightly to mix.
2. Strain into a small glass. Hang the strip of orange peel over the rim of the glass so that one end is in the cocktail.

Macaulay

Serves 1
Preparation time: 5 minutes

cracked ice

1 measure Cognac

1 measure dry vermouth

2 measures Curacao

strip of orange peel, to decorate

1. Place some cracked ice, the Cognac, vermouth and Curacao in a cocktail shaker or screw-topped jar. Shake to mix.
2. Strain into a tall glass.
3. Place the strip of orange in the glass.

Manhattan

Serves 1
Preparation time: 5 minutes

cracked ice

2 measures rye whisky

1 measure sweet vermouth

dash of Angostura bitters

To decorate:

1 cocktail cherry

strip of lemon peel

1. Put some cracked ice into a glass.
2. Mix together the whisky, vermouth and bitters, then pour over the ice.
3. Stir once. Add the cherry and lemon peel on a cocktail stick, to decorate.

Variation: A dry version can be made by using dry vermouth instead of sweet.

Martini

Serves 1
Preparation time: 5 minutes

For a Dry Martini:

cracked ice

1 measure gin

2 measures dry vermouth

To decorate:

strip of lemon peel

1 green olive

For a Sweet Martini:

few drops of orange bitters (optional)

2 measures gin

1 measure sweet vermouth

1 cocktail cherry, to decorate

1. Put some cracked ice in a glass.
2. Pour the gin and vermouth over and stir. Hang the strip of lemon peel over the rim of the glass so that one end is in the cocktail or place it in the glass.
3. Add the olive.

1. Shake a few drops of bitters into a glass and swirl it round to coat the sides.
2. Add the gin and vermouth, and stir to mix. Decorate with the cherry.

Negroni

Serves 1
Preparation time: 5 minutes

1 measure dry gin

1 measure sweet vermouth

1 measure Campari

cracked ice

½ slice orange

soda water (optional)

1. Place the gin, vermouth and Campari in a tumbler. Stir to mix.
2. Add some cracked ice, the orange slice and soda water to taste, if using.

Old-fashioned

Serves 1
Preparation time: 5 minutes

1 sugar lump

1-2 drops Angostura bitters

1-2 ice cubes

1 measure whisky

½ slice orange

1. Put the sugar into a tumbler, shake in the bitters and stir until the sugar has dissolved.
2. Add the ice cubes and stir to coat with the liquid.
3. Add the whisky, stir lightly then float the orange slice on top.

Pimms

Serves 1
Preparation time: 5 minutes

ice cubes

50 ml/2 fl oz Pimms

175 ml/6 fl oz lemonade, chilled

sprig of mint or borage (optional)

strip of cucumber rind (optional)

slice of apple, orange and lemon (optional)

1. Put some ice cubes into a tall glass. Pour over the Pimms and stir.
2. Top up with lemonade.
3. Float the mint or borage, cucumber rind and fruit slices on top, if using.

Pina colada

Serves 1
Preparation time: 5 minutes

cracked ice

1 measure white rum

2 measures cream of coconut milk

2 measures fresh pineapple juice

To decorate:

1 slice orange

1 cocktail cherry

slice of canned or fresh pineapple

1. Place some cracked ice, the rum, cream of coconut milk and pineapple in a cocktail shaker or screw-topped jar. Shake lightly to mix.
2. Strain into a large glass and decorate with the fruit.

Pink gin

Serves 1
Preparation time: 5 minutes

1-4 drops Angostura bitters

1 measure gin

iced water

1. Shake the bitters into a cocktail glass and roll it around until the sides are well coated.
2. Add the gin, then iced water to taste.

Screwdriver

Serves 1
Preparation time: 5 minutes

2-3 ice cubes

1 measure vodka

juice of 1 orange

1. Put the ice cubes into a tumbler.
2. Add the vodka and orange juice, and stir lightly.

Snowball

Serves 1
Preparation time: 5 minutes

lightly beaten egg white

caster sugar

cracked ice

1 measure advocaat

dash of lime juice or cordial

lemonade

To decorate:

1 cocktail cherry

1 slice orange

1. Dip the rim of a glass in lightly beaten egg white, then in caster sugar.
2. Put some cracked ice into the glass. Add the advocaat and lime juice, and stir to mix.
3. Top up with lemonade to taste. Decorate with the cherry and orange slice.

Soleil rouge

Serves 1
Preparation time: 5 minutes

1 measure dry sherry
1 measure St. Raphael rouge
3 dashes Angostura bitters
1 strip of orange peel, twisted

1. Stir together the sherry, St. Raphael and Angostura bitters in a glass.
2. Hang the strip of orange peel over the rim of the glass so that one end is in the cocktail.

Stockers

Serves 1
Preparation time: 5 minutes

lightly beaten egg white
caster sugar
cracked ice
2 measures Cognac
1 measure crème de menthe
soda water

1. Dip the rim of a glass in lightly beaten egg white, then in caster sugar.
2. Place some cracked ice, the Cognac and crème de menthe in a cocktail shaker or screw-topped jar. Shake lightly to mix.
3. Strain into the glass and top up with soda water to taste.

Whisky sour

Serves 1
Preparation time: 5 minutes

2-3 teaspoons lemon juice
1 teaspoon caster sugar
cracked ice
1 measure whisky

1. In a whisky tumbler stir together the lemon juice and caster sugar, until the sugar has dissolved.
2. Add some cracked ice and stir to coat with the liquid.
3. Add the whisky and stir lightly.

White lady

Serves 1
Preparation time: 5 minutes

2 measures gin

1 measure Cointreau

1 teaspoon lemon juice

about ½ teaspoon egg white

1. Place the gin, Cointreau, lemon juice and egg white in a cocktail shaker or screw-topped jar. Shake to mix.
2. Strain into a cocktail glass.

Zandaria

Serves 1
Preparation time: 5 minutes

cracked ice

1 measure Cognac

1 measure Tia Maria

1 measure double cream

pinch of grated nutmeg
    (optional)

1. Place some cracked ice, the Cognac, Tia Maria and cream in a cocktail shaker or screw-topped jar. Shake lightly to mix.
2. Strain into a cocktail glass, or pour straight into the glass. Grated nutmeg can be sprinkled over the top.

Zed

Serves 1
Preparation time: 5 minutes

cracked ice

1 measure gin

1 measure Mandarine Napoléon
    liqueur

3 measures fresh pineapple
    juice

1 teaspoon sugar

To decorate:

1 slice lemon, cut in half

sprig of mint

1. Place some cracked ice, the gin, liqueur, pineapple juice and sugar in a cocktail shaker or screw-topped jar. Shake lightly to mix.
2. Strain into a small tumbler. Decorate with the slice of lemon and mint.

Fruit sparkler

Makes about 18-20 glasses
Preparation time: 5 minutes

2 x 70 cl/24.64 fl oz bottles
  Riesling, chilled

50 ml/2 fl oz brandy

1 x 75 cl/26.40 fl oz bottle
  sparkling white wine, chilled

225 g/8 oz fresh fruit, e.g.,
  hulled raspberries or
  strawberries, sliced peaches,
  melon balls or cubes

1. Pour the Riesling into a large jug or divide between 2 jugs.
2. Stir in the brandy then add the sparkling wine, dividing them both appropriately if 2 jugs have been used.
3. Add the fruit.

Bucks fizz

Preparation time: 5 minutes

1 part fresh orange juice,
  chilled

1 part champagne, chilled

Any size of glass can be used – a 300 ml/ 1/2 pint is a good size – but remember when calculating amounts, the glass cannot actually be filled as room has to be left for the bubbling of the champagne.
Bucks Fizz can also be made in a jug.

1. Pour some orange juice into a chilled glass or a jug.
2. Top up with an equal amount of champagne.

Kir royale

Serves 1
Preparation time: 5 minutes

1 teaspoon Crème de Cassis

150-175 ml/5-6 fl oz champagne,
   chilled

1. Measure the Cassis into a chilled tall slim glass or champagne flute.
2. Pour in the champagne and stir until just blended.

Cherry fizz

Makes about 8-10 glasses
Preparation time: 5 minutes, plus chilling

85 ml/3 fl oz double cream

135 ml/4½ fl oz cherry brandy

3 tablespoons white rum

1 x 75 cl/26.40 fl oz bottle
   sparkling white wine, chilled

To decorate:

lightly beaten egg white

caster sugar

mint leaves

1. Mix together the double cream, cherry brandy and white rum in a jug. Chill well.
2. Gradually pour in the sparkling wine, stirring at first to blend together. Add the mint.
3. Give a final stir just before serving. Pour into glasses which have had the rims dipped in lightly beaten egg white then caster sugar.
4. Decorate with the mint.

Variation: Pineapple Fizz. Use 135 ml/ 4½ fl oz from a carton of fresh pineapple juice instead of the cherry brandy.

Black velvet

Preparation time: 5 minutes

1 part Guinness, chilled

1 part champagne, chilled

Any size of glass can be used — 300 ml/½ pint and 600 ml/1 pint goblets are particularly suitable — but remember when calculating amounts, the glass cannot be filled as room has to be left for the 'head'. Black Velvet can also be made in a jug.

1. Carefully pour some Guinness into a chilled glass.
2. Carefully pour in an equal amount of champagne.

Champagne cup

Makes about 8 glasses
Preparation time: 5 minutes

ice

4 tablespoons Cognac

1½ tablespoons apricot liqueur

2 tablespoons Curaçao

1 x 75 cl/26.40 fl oz bottle
  champagne,
  chilled

fresh seasonal fruit

1. Put some ice in a large, chilled jug.
2. Measure in the Cognac and liqueurs, and stir well.
3. Carefully pour in the champagne and stir once or twice to mix evenly.
4. Place a little fruit in each glass and pour the sparkling drink over.

Sherry punch

Makes 12-13 glasses
Preparation time: 10 minutes

ice cubes

1 x 70 cl/24.64 fl oz bottle
medium sherry, chilled

1 x 75 cl/26.40 fl oz bottle
lemonade, chilled

50 ml/2 fl oz Mandarine
Napoléon liqueur

cucumber slices

1 eating apple, sliced

1 orange, sliced

sprig of mint

1. Put some ice cubes in a chilled large bowl and pour the sherry, lemonade and liqueur, if using, over.
2. Add the cucumber, fruit and mint. Serve as soon as possible.

Planter's punch

Makes about 8 glasses (if undiluted)
Preparation time: 10 minutes, plus
2 hours for chilling

100 g/4 oz caster sugar

8 tablespoons water

120 ml/4 fl oz lime juice

1 x 75 cl/26.40 fl oz bottle
white rum

few drops of Angostura bitters

ice cubes

lime, lemon and orange slices

Maraschino cherries

soda water (optional)

1. Gently dissolve the sugar in the water in a small saucepan.
2. Pour into a cocktail shaker or a bottle, add the lime juice, rum and bitters, and shake well. Chill for 2 hours.
3. Put some ice cubes into a jug, pour the punch over and add the fruit.
4. Dilute with soda water to taste, if preferred.

Tea punch

Makes about 8 glasses
Preparation time: 20 minutes, plus 10 minutes for infusing and 2 hours for chilling

600 ml/1 pint China tea

100 g/4 oz sugar

juice of 2 lemons

juice of 1 orange

1 small vanilla pod

1 x 5 cm/2 inch cinnamon stick

150 ml/¼ pint brandy

150 ml/¼ pint dark rum

50 ml/2 fl oz Grand Marnier
(optional)

about 300 ml/½ pint soda water,
chilled

1 orange, sliced

1 lemon, sliced

Maraschino cherries

1. Leave the tea to infuse for 10 minutes, then strain into a saucepan. Add the sugar and heat gently until dissolved.
2. Add the fruit juices, vanilla pod, cinnamon stick, brandy and rum, and heat gently to just below simmering for 5 minutes.
3. Leave until cold, then chill for 2 hours.
4. Remove the vanilla pod and cinnamon stick. Add the Grand Marnier, if using, and top up with soda water to taste.
5. Float the fruit on top.

Red wine cup

Makes 12-14 glasses
Preparation time: 10 minutes, plus
2 hours for chilling

50 g/2 oz sugar

75 ml/3 fl oz water

juice of 2 oranges

2 x 75 cl/26.40 fl oz bottles
    medium light red wine

175 ml/6 fl oz dry vermouth

about 300 ml/½ pint lemonade,
    chilled

thin strips of orange rind

cucumber slices

borage, if available

1. Gently dissolve the sugar in the water in a small saucepan, then leave to cool.
2. Pour the wine into a bowl, add the cold sugar syrup and the vermouth. Chill for 2 hours.
3. Just before serving, add the lemonade, orange rind, cucumber and borage.

Oxford cup

Makes 10-12 glasses
Preparation time: 10 minutes, plus
30 minutes for soaking and 1 hour for
chilling

1 lemon, thinly sliced

1 orange, thinly sliced

about 2 tablespoons brown
    sugar, to taste

large pinch of grated nutmeg

1 litre/1¾ pints strong ale

1 x 70 cl/24.64 fl oz bottle dry
    white wine

4 slices toast

1. Put the fruit in a large jug and sprinkle the sugar and nutmeg over.
2. Leave for 30 minutes.
3. Pour the ale and wine over, and add the toast. Cover and chill for 1 hour.
4. Strain before serving.

Rosé cup

Makes 12-14 glasses
Preparation time: 5 minutes

ice cubes

1 x 75 cl/26.40 fl oz bottle
rose wine, chilled

1 x 70cl/24.64 fl oz bottle
sweet white wine, chilled

4 tablespoons Southern Comfort

450 ml/³⁄₄ pint tonic water,
chilled

about 4 tablespoons canned
mandarin segments

1. Put the ice in a chilled large bowl and pour the wines, Southern Comfort and tonic water over.
2. Add the fruit and sufficient of their syrup to taste. Serve as soon as possible.

Summer cup

Makes about 15 glasses
Preparation time: 5 minutes

1 x 70 cl/24.64 fl oz bottle
Riesling, chilled

1 x 75 cl/26.40 fl oz bottle
light red wine

75 ml/3 fl oz Drambuie

750 ml/1 ¼ pints lemonade,
chilled

1 eating apple, sliced

1 orange, sliced

few fresh strawberries, halved

ice cubes

1. Pour the wines and Drambuie into a chilled large bowl.
2. Add the lemonade, fruit and ice cubes. Serve as soon as possible.

White wine cup

Makes 10-12 glasses
Preparation time: 10 minutes, plus
2½ hours for chilling

3 apricots or 1 peach, sliced
  (optional)

some fresh blackcurrants or
  strawberries

1 tablespoon caster sugar

75 ml/3 fl oz (or 1 miniature)
  Cointreau

1 x 70 cl/24.64 fl oz bottle
  medium dry white wine

1 x 70 cl/24.64 fl oz bottle
  Riesling

1. Put the fruit in a large bowl and sprinkle the sugar over. Chill for 30 minutes.
2. Add the Cointreau and wine. Chill for 2 hours.

Honeysuckle cup

Makes 10-12 glasses
Preparation time: 10 minutes, plus
2 hours for chilling

1 tablespoon clear honey

1 x 75 cl/26.40 fl oz bottle
  medium dry white wine

2 tablespoons Benedictine

150 ml/¼ pint brandy

750 ml/1¼ pints lemonade,
  chilled

1 peach, sliced

few fresh raspberries or
  strawberries

1. Put the honey in a large bowl and gradually stir in the wine.
2. Add the Benedictine and brandy. Chill for 2 hours.
3. Just before serving, add the lemonade and fruit.

Sangria

Makes 11-12 glasses
Preparation time: 10 minutes

ice cubes

2 x 75 cl/26.40 fl oz bottles
　　Spanish red wine, chilled

120 ml/4 fl oz brandy
　　(optional)

about 450 ml/¾ pint soda water,
　　chilled

sliced seasonal fruit, e.g.,
　　apples, pears, oranges,
　　lemons, peaches

1. Put some ice into a large bowl and pour the wine and brandy, if using, over. Stir.
2. Add soda water to taste and float the sliced fruit on top.

Boatman's cup

Makes 14-15 glasses
Preparation time: 10 minutes, plus
2 hours for chilling

1 x 70 cl/24.64 fl oz bottle
　　Riesling

500 ml/18 fl oz still dry cider

75 ml/3 fl oz brandy

about 175 ml/6 fl oz frozen
　　orange juice concentrate,
　　thawed

750 ml/1¼ pints lemonade,
　　chilled

few black cherries, halved

1 slice orange

melon balls or cubes

sprigs of mint

1. Mix together the wine, cider, brandy and orange juice. Chill for 2 hours.
2. Just before serving, add the lemonade, fruit and mint.

Mulled Madeira

Makes 10-12 glasses or mugs
Preparation time: 20 minutes

1 x 70 cl/24.64 fl oz bottle bual
  (sweet) Madeira

4 tablespoons brandy

4 tablespoons apricot brandy

300 ml/½ pint fresh orange
  juice

about 150 ml/¼ pint hot water

grated nutmeg

1. Gently heat the Madeira, brandies and orange juice in a saucepan to just below simmering point for 10 minutes.
2. Add hot water to taste and serve in warmed glasses or mugs. Sprinkle nutmeg over the top.

Mulled red wine (1)

Makes about 6 glasses or mugs
Preparation time: 35 minutes

large pinch of ground ginger

1 tablespoon brown sugar

8 cloves

150 ml/¼ pint water

1 x 75 cl/26.40 fl oz bottle red
  wine

150 ml/¼ pint port

1. Mix the ginger with the sugar in a saucepan, then gently simmer with the cloves and water for 20 minutes. Strain.
2. Gently heat with the wine for 5 minutes to just below simmering point.
3. Add the port. Serve in warmed glasses or mugs.

Glögg

Makes 8-10 glasses or mugs
Preparation time: 20 minutes

75 g/3 oz sugar

1 x 75 cl/26.40 fl oz bottle brandy

12 cloves

pinch of ground cinnamon

pinch of grated nutmeg

50 g/2 oz large raisins

50 g/2 oz unsalted blanched
  almonds

1 litre/1¾ pints medium sweet
  sherry

1. Gently dissolve the sugar in the brandy in a saucepan. Add the cloves, cinnamon, nutmeg, raisins and almonds, and heat to just below simmering point for 10 minutes.
2. Heat the sherry separately to just below simmering point.
3. Ignite the brandy mixture and pour in the sherry.
4. Serve immediately in warmed glasses or mugs.

Mulled red wine (2)

Makes about 8-10 glasses
Preparation time: 25 minutes
Cooking time: 30 minutes
Oven: 190°C, 375°F, Gas Mark 5

1 orange

1 lemon, thickly sliced

8 cloves

2 bay leaves

1 x 5 cm/2 inch cinnamon stick

75 g/3 oz sugar

2 x 75 cl/26.40 fl oz bottles red
  wine

120 ml/4 fl oz brandy

1. Place the orange in a preheated oven and bake for 30 minutes.
2. Put the orange, lemon slices, cloves, bay leaves, half the sugar and the wine into a saucepan. Gradually heat to just below simmering point and continue to heat for 20 minutes.
3. Gently dissolve the remaining sugar in the brandy in a small saucepan.
4. Strain the wine into a warmed heatproof bowl. Ignite the brandy and let it flame for a few seconds before pouring into the wine.
5. Serve immediately in warmed glasses.

Polish honey drink

Makes about 8 glasses or mugs
Preparation time: 20 minutes, plus
1 hour for infusing

about 6 tablespoons clear honey

300 ml/½ pint water

4 cloves

1 x 7.5 cm/3 inch cinnamon
    stick

1 vanilla pod

2 long strips lemon rind

2 long strips orange rind

1 x 75 cl/26.40 fl oz bottle vodka

1. Gently melt the honey in the water in a saucepan. Add the cloves, cinnamon stick, vanilla pod and fruit rinds, bring to the boil and simmer for 5 minutes.
2. Cover, remove from the heat and leave to infuse for 1 hour.
3. Strain and return to the cleaned pan. Add the vodka and gently heat to just below simmering point for 5 minutes.
4. Serve in modest amounts in warmed glasses or mugs.

Rum punch

Makes 9-10 mugs or glasses
Preparation time: 15 minutes, plus
1 hour for infusing

12 sugar lumps

2 oranges

2 lemons

1 litre/1¾ pints water

8 cloves

1 x 7.5 cm/3 inch cinnamon
    stick

600 ml/1 pint dark rum

1. Rub the sugar lumps over the rind of 1 orange and 1 lemon to remove the zest.
2. Gently dissolve the sugar in the water in a saucepan.
3. Add the cloves and cinnamon stick, and boil steadily for 5 minutes.
4. Remove from the heat and add the rum. Cover and leave to infuse for 1 hour.
5. Squeeze the orange and the lemon which have had the zest removed. Slice the remaining orange and lemon.
6. Strain the punch, pour into a clean pan, and add the fruit juice. Reheat gently to just below simmering point.
7. Float the remaining fruit on top and serve in warmed mugs or glasses.

Mulled white wine

Makes about 6 glasses or mugs
Preparation time: 15 minutes

1 lemon

4 tablespoons clear honey

1 x 5 cm/2 inch cinnamon stick

1 x 70 cl/24.64 fl oz bottle
    medium dry white wine

4 tablespoons whisky

1 orange, sliced

1. Thinly pare the rind from the lemon and squeeze the juice.

2. Mix the juice with the honey in a saucepan. Add the rind, cinnamon stick and wine, and heat gently to just below simmering point for 10 minutes. Remove the cinnamon stick.

3. Add the whisky and sliced orange.

4. Serve in warmed glasses or mugs.

Mulled ale (Lamb's wool)

Makes 10-12 mugs
Preparation time: 10 minutes
Cooking time: about 40 minutes
Oven: 180°C, 350°F, Gas Mark 4

6 cooking apples

36 cloves

large pinch of grated nutmeg

25 g/1 oz soft brown sugar

20 g/³⁄₄ oz unsalted butter

600 ml/1 pint sweet white wine

1 litre/1³⁄₄ pints strong ale

1. Spike the apples with the cloves. Place in a preheated oven and bake for about 40 minutes until very soft.

2. Scoop out the flesh and beat in the nutmeg, sugar and butter.

3. Gently heat the wine and ale in a saucepan to just below simmering point. Float the apple mixture on top.

4. Ladle into warmed glasses or mugs and serve with spoons.

The bishop

Makes 10-12 glasses or mugs
Preparation time: 20 minutes
Cooking time: 20 minutes
Oven: 180°C, 350°F, Gas Mark 4

10 cloves

1 orange

1 lemon

50 g/2 oz lump sugar

1½ x 70 cl/24.64 fl oz bottles port

600 ml/1 pint boiling water

1 x 5 cm/2 inch cinnamon stick

pinch of grated nutmeg

1. Spike the cloves into the orange. Place in a preheated oven and bake for 20 minutes.
2. Rub the rind of the lemon with the sugar to remove the zest, and reserve. Squeeze the juice.
3. Put the baked orange into a large saucepan and add the port, boiling water, cinnamon stick and nutmeg. Gently heat to just below simmering point for 10 minutes.
4. Add the sugar cubes and lemon juice. Serve immediately in warmed glasses or mugs.

Mulled beer

Makes 8-10 glasses or mugs
Preparation time: 20 minutes

about 2 tablespoons honey, to taste

large pinch of ground ginger

1 litre/1¾ pints beer

300 ml/½ pint sweet sherry

long strip of lemon peel

1 eating apple, thinly sliced

grated nutmeg

1. Gently melt the honey with the ginger in a saucepan, then stir in the beer and sherry.
2. Add the lemon peel, gradually heat to just below simmering point and continue to heat for 10 minutes.
3. Float the apple slices on top and sprinkle with nutmeg. Serve in warmed glasses or mugs.

Café brûlot

Serves 1
Preparation time: 5 minutes

small strip of finely pared
   orange rind

1 x 2.5 cm/1 inch cinnamon
   stick

1 clove

1 teaspoon brown sugar

175 ml/6 fl oz strong black coffee

2 tablespoons Cognac

1. Put the orange rind, cinnamon stick, clove, sugar and coffee in a small saucepan and gradually bring to just below boiling point.
2. Strain into a warmed coffee cup or glass.
3. Warm the Cognac in a soup ladle, ignite and pour, flaming, into the coffee.

Sweet dreams

Serves 1
Preparation time: 5 minutes

250 ml/8 fl oz hot milk

70 ml/2½ fl oz Tia Maria

pinch of grated nutmeg

1. Pour the milk into a warmed cup or glass' then stir in the Tia Maria.
2. Sprinkle the nutmeg over the top.

Apple posset

Serves 1
Preparation time: 5 minutes

200 ml/⅓ pint unsweetened
   apple juice

1 teaspoon soft brown sugar

2 tablespoons Calvados

1 x 5 cm/2 inch cinnamon stick

1. Heat the apple juice in a small saucepan to just below boiling point.
2. Meanwhile, measure the sugar and Calvados into a warmed mug or glass.
3. Pour the hot apple juice on to the Calvados, stirring with the cinnamon stick until the sugar has dissolved.

Buttered rum

Serves 1
Preparation time: 5 minutes

50 ml/2 fl oz Cognac
1½ teaspoons soft brown sugar
200 ml/⅓ pint boiling water
15 g/½ oz unsalted butter
pinch of grated nutmeg

1. Measure the Cognac, sugar and 50 ml/2 fl oz of the water into a warmed cup, mug or glass. Add the butter and stir until melted.
2. Add the remaining water and sprinkle the nutmeg over the top.

Egg nog

Serves 1
Preparation time: 5 minutes

300 ml/½ pint milk
1 egg
1 tablespoon soft brown sugar
50 ml/2 fl oz Cognac
pinch of grated nutmeg

1. Heat the milk in a small saucepan to just below boiling point.
2. Meanwhile, whisk the egg and sugar together in a small basin then whisk in the Cognac.
3. Whisk in the hot milk then pour into a warmed mug, cup or glass. Sprinkle the nutmeg over the top.

Moonrise

Serves 1
Preparation time: 5 minutes

large pinch of grated nutmeg

large pinch of ground cinnamon

about 1 tablespoon brown sugar

300 ml/½ pint medium dry cider

2 tablespoons Calvados

1 dessertspoon double cream

1. Mix the nutmeg and cinnamon with the sugar.
2. Warm the cider with the spice and sugar mixture in a saucepan but do not boil. Add a little more sugar if preferred.
3. Stir in the Calvados and pour into a warmed glass or mug.
4. Float the cream on top.

Apple and cider cup

Makes about 14 glasses
Preparation time: 10 minutes plus chilling

1 litre/1¾ pints apple juice

rind of 1 lemon, cut into strips

1 piece fresh root ginger

about 25 g/1 oz brown sugar

120 ml/4 fl oz Nassau Orange
   Liqueur

3 dessert apples, cored and sliced

2 litres/3½ pints dry cider,
   chilled

1. Gently heat the apple juice, lemon rind, ginger and sugar in a saucepan for 2-3 minutes but do not allow to boil. Add a little more sugar if preferred. Leave to cool.
2. Stir in the liqueur and 2 of the apples. Leave until cold, then chill.
3. Add the cider and remaining apple.

Sinking sun

Serves 1
Preparation time: 5 minutes

1 tablespoon crushed ice

strip of lemon peel

2 tablespoons whisky

175 ml/6 fl oz dry cider

1. Put the ice and lemon peel into a tumbler.
2. Pour the whisky over and stir well.
3. Pour in the cider and stir to mix.

Mulled cider punch

Makes about 15 glasses
Preparation time: 35 minutes
Cooking time: 20 minutes
Oven: 180°C, 350°F, Gas Mark 4

1 orange

1 lemon

12 cloves

150 ml/¼ pint water

3 tablespoons clear honey, or to taste

1 x 5 cm/2 inch cinnamon stick

2.75 litres/5 pints medium dry cider

175 ml/6 fl oz brandy

1. Stud the orange and lemon with the cloves. Place in a preheated oven and bake for 20 minutes.
2. Gently heat the water, honey and cinnamon stick in a large saucepan until the honey has dissolved. Add the orange and lemon, and heat gently for 5-10 minutes but do not allow to boil.
3. Add the brandy and warm gently before serving in warmed glasses.

Raisin & ginger punch

Makes 6-7 glasses
Preparation time: 10 minutes, plus
several hours for infusing

rind and juice of 1 lemon

1 tablespoon clear honey

50 g/2 oz plump raisins

ice cubes

600 ml/1 pint apple juice

1 orange, peeled

1 apple

600 ml/1 pint ginger ale

sprigs of mint

1. Mix together the lemon rind and juice, honey and raisins in a tall jug and leave, covered, for several hours.
2. Stir in some ice cubes then the apple juice.
3. Remove the pith from the orange and divide into segments, cutting away all the skin and membrane. Core the apple and cut into segments.
4. Pour the ginger ale into the punch. Float the segments of orange, apple and the mint on top.

Mulled fruit punch

Makes 7-8 glasses or mugs
Preparation time: 10 minutes, plus
2-3 hours for infusing

2-3 tablespoons brown sugar

6 tablespoons fresh orange juice

3 tablespoons lemon juice

1 litre/1¾ pints apple juice

12 cloves

1 x 5 cm/2 inch cinnamon stick

1 apple

1 lemon, sliced

1. Dissolve the sugar in the orange, lemon and apple juices. Add the cloves and cinnamon stick, and gradually heat to just below boiling point.
2. Remove from the heat, cover and leave to infuse for 2-3 hours.
3. Just before serving, core the apple and divide into segments.
4. Heat the punch gently to just below simmering point. Remove the cinnamon stick and add the apple and lemon. Serve in warmed glasses or mugs.

Citrus punch

Makes 8-9 glasses
Preparation time: 5 minutes, plus
2 hours for chilling

600 ml/1 pint fresh orange juice

600 ml/1 pint fresh grapefruit
  juice

ice cubes

450 ml/¾ pint lemonade, chilled

To decorate:

1 lemon, sliced

1 orange, sliced

cocktail cherries (optional)

1. Mix the orange and grapefruit juices together and chill for 2 hours.
2. Stir in some ice cubes and add the lemonade. Decorate with the slices of lemon, orange and the cherries, if using.

Red mademoiselle

Serves 1
Preparation time: 5 minutes

lightly beaten egg white

caster sugar

1½ tablespoons redcurrant jelly

3 tablespoons vanilla ice cream

175 ml/6 fl oz soda water, or to
  taste

1. Dip the rim of a tall glass in the egg white then caster sugar.
2. Whisk together the redcurrant jelly, ice cream and half the soda water, or mix in a blender.
3. Pour into the glass and top up with soda water to taste.

Melon cup

Makes 5-6 glasses
Preparation time: 10 minutes

450 g/1 lb flesh from cantaloupe
  or ogen melon

about 1 tablespoon caster sugar

rind of 2 lemons and 3
  tablespoons lemon juice

few dashes of Grenadine

600 ml 1 pint soda water, or to
  taste, chilled

mint leaves, to decorate
  (optional)

1. Purée or pass the melon flesh through a sieve. Put into a large jug.
2. Gently dissolve the sugar with the lemon juice and rind. Pour into the melon purée with the Grenadine and mix thoroughly. Chill.
3. Just before serving add the soda water and decorate with mint leaves, if using.

Note

1. Preparation times given are an average calculated during recipe testing.

2. Metric and imperial measurements have been calculated separately. Use one set of measurements only as they are not exact equivalents.

3. Spoon measures can be bought in both imperial and metric sizes to give accurate measurement of small quantities. All spoon measurements are level.

4. To warm glasses immerse them in, or fill them with, hot but not boiling water. Empty and dry them.

To warm mugs, immerse them in boiling water. Leave for a few minutes, then pour out and dry.

5. To prepare cracked ice, put some ice in a strong polythene bag. Bring down sharply on a firm surface, or crack with a heavy implement, such as a wooden rolling pin. Alternatively, use a food processor.

Acknowledgements
Photography: Bryce Attwell
Photographic styling: Lesley Richardson
Preparation of drinks for photography: Caroline Ellwood

The publishers would like to thank the following for the loan of props for photography:
Christopher Wray, 593 King's Road, London SW6; Coconut Grove, Barrett Street, London W1; Evergreens, 36 Drury Lane, London WC2; Practical Styling, Centre Point, 16-18 St Giles Street, London WC2; Strangeways, 502 King's Road, London SW10; The Cocktail Shop, Avery Row, London W1; William Page, 91 Shaftesbury Avenue, London W1; World's End Nurseries, 441/457 King's Road, London SW10; Zanzibar, 30 Great Queen Street, London WC2.

The publishers would also like to thank the following for their kindness in supplying alcohol for photography:
Red wine and claret from Grants of St. James's; Sherry from Harveys of Bristol; Port from Cockburn's; Drambuie, Galliano, sweet and dry vermouth from Atkinson Baldwin & Company; Bacardi rum from Bacardi International Limited; Apricot brandy, crème de cassis, cherry brandy and Cointreau from Cointreau & Regnier Liqueurs; Sweet and dry vermouth from Cinzano (UK) Ltd; and some help from Peter Dominic.

First published in 1982 by
Octopus Books Limited
59 Grosvenor Street, London W1
© 1982 Hennerwood Publications Limited

ISBN 0 86273 036 8

Produced by Mandarin Publishers Limited
Printed in Hong Kong